T0287590

BRISTOL RE BUSES AND COACHES

ROBERT APPLETON

AMBERLEY

First published 2020

Amberley Publishing
The Hill, Stroud
Gloucestershire, GL5 4EP

www.amberley-books.com

Copyright © Robert Appleton, 2020

The right of Robert Appleton to be identified
as the Author of this work has been asserted in
accordance with the Copyrights, Designs and
Patents Act 1988.

ISBN 978 1 4456 9585 3 (print)
ISBN 978 1 4456 9586 0 (ebook)

British Library Cataloguing in Publication Data.
A catalogue record for this book is available from
the British Library.

Origination by Amberley Publishing.
Printed in the UK.

Introduction

In 1961 the maximum length of single-deckers was increased to 36 feet. Bristol Commercial Vehicles and Eastern Coach Works designed their first rear-engined single-decker to take advantage of this new length.

The engine used was the Gardner 6HLX, mounted immediately behind the double reduction rear axle derived from the Bristol Lodekka. This enabled the drive to be taken forward to the syncromesh gearbox, then back to the axle. This arrangement improved weight distribution. Brakes were air-hydraulic, and there was air suspension on both axles.

Two prototypes were built and tested in service in 1962. United Automobile Services had BR1 (7431 HN) the RELL6G version for bus work. South Midland had 867 (521 ABL) the RELH6G version for coachwork. A third prototype, another RELH6G, was kept by Bristol Commercial Vehicles as a test rig. This became West Yorkshire Road Car CRG1 (OWT 241E) in 1967. The Bristol chassis code RELL6G meant 'rear engine long length low frame Gardner 6-cylinder engine', and RELH6G meant 'rear engine long length high frame Gardner 6-cylinder engine'.

The low frame for bus use gave shallow steps at the front entrance, and a gentle sloping floor. The high frame for coach use gave higher steps, a flat floor, side luggage lockers, and a rear boot.

Production started in 1963, with Eastern Coach Works-bodied buses and coaches for the nationalised Tilling Group companies, plus some Alexander-bodied coaches for the nationalised Scottish Motor Traction Group companies.

In 1966 Leyland took a 25 per cent share in Bristol Commercial Vehicles and Eastern Coach Works, allowing them to return to the open market. To widen the appeal of the Bristol RE, a revised series 2 model was introduced. For the RELL and RELH, the wheelbase was reduced from 19 feet to 18 feet 6 inches to give a wider front entrance on bus versions. RESL and RESH versions, with 16 feet 2 inch wheelbase for bodywork up to 32 feet in length, were introduced. Engine options were: Gardner 6HLW 8.4 litres, Gardner 6HLX 10.45 litres, Leyland 0.600H 9.8 litres and Leyland 0.680H 11.1 litres. Brakes were changed to full air. Standard suspension was leaf spring, with air suspension as an option. Syncromesh transmission was standard, with semi-automatic as an option.

In practice, Gardner 6HLX and Leyland 0.680H became the most common engines. Semi-automatic transmission was adopted by nearly all operators, to aid one-person operation. In contrast most operators specified the standard leaf spring suspension, and only a minority took air suspension.

With Bristol back on the open market, other body builders could body the Bristol RE. These included Alexander, East Lancashire, Marshall, Northern Counties, Park Royal, Pennine, and Plaxton. The series 2 Bristol RE was very successful, becoming the standard single-decker with many Tilling companies within the National Bus Company. The Bristol RE was also bought by some of the ex-British Electric Traction companies within the National Bus Company, as well as several municipal operators.

In 1968 the REMH version was launched with a 20 feet wheelbase for 39 feet 4 inches (12 metres) long coach bodywork.

In 1970 the RESL was revised with a 16 feet 6 inch wheelbase for 33 feet (10 metres) long bodywork. On Eastern Coach Works-bodied examples, this version can be recognised by the thick pillar behind the driver's cab window, and slightly longer window bays.

The ECW bus body went through some changes. In 1967 a flat windscreen with peaked domes, front and rear, was introduced. In 1969 a taller flat windscreen was adopted. Then, in 1970, the British Electric Traction-style curved windscreen design was introduced. This increased the overall length from 36 feet 1 inch to 36 feet 5 inches on the Bristol RELL.

1968 to 1972 were the peak production years for the Bristol RE. However, the introduction of the Leyland National in 1972 meant that National Bus Company subsidiaries were directed to buy the Leyland National instead of the Bristol RELL for bus work. They were allowed to buy the Bristol RELH for coach and express service work in 1973 and 1974. The Bristol RESL and RELL remained popular with municipal operators but, despite this, Leyland withdrew the Bristol RE from the home market in 1975.

The Bristol RE remained in production for export markets. The term export was interpreted to include Northern Ireland, so orders were accepted from Ulsterbus and Citybus for 600 Bristol RELL6Gs with Alexander (Belfast) bodies built from 1975 to 1983. True export orders were received from the Christchurch Transport Board, in New Zealand, for ninety-eight Bristol RELL6Ls with Leyland 510 engines, bodied locally by Hawke or New Zealand Motor Bodies. Production of the Bristol RE finally ceased in 1983.

My first sighting of a Bristol RE was on a summer evening in 1967, when Eastern Counties RS648 (KVF 648E) went past the family home in Harwich Road, Mistley, working on service 123 from Ipswich to Clacton. RS648 was one of fourteen Bristol RESL6G with ECW bodies new in 1967. These had five-speed manual gearboxes.

Then, in 1968, Eastern Counties received twenty Bristol RELL6Gs with ECW bodies and five-speed semi-automatic gearboxes, RL665–684, with RL679/680 (RAH 679/680F) allocated to Ipswich. I had many journeys on RL679/680, and later RLs in the Eastern Counties fleet. So, what was it like to travel on one of these? As the RL pulls up at the bus stop, note the wide entrance and shallow steps, which made boarding and alighting so much easier than on an underfloor mid-engined single-decker, then the inward-facing bench seats over the front wheel arches. The saloon floor gently slopes up to the rear, and there are no more steps to negotiate. As the RL accelerates away, upward gear changes can be made early due to the good torque of the Gardner 6HLX engine. The driver pauses the gear selector in neutral during gear changes to give a smooth change and reduce the wear on the transmission. Very soon we are cruising along in fifth gear, accompanied by the low noise of the Gardner engine, and a melodious whine from the transmission. The ECW body does not rattle, except for the glass panel behind the driver's cab on some RLs. Eastern Counties' drivers solved this by wedging a roll of unused Setright tickets between the glass panel and a stanchion!

I found the semi-coach seats in Eastern Counties' RLE classes to be very comfortable, and even ECW's standard bus seats were more comfortable than the seats on many modern buses.

A long bus journey on a Bristol RELL or RELH was always good. Among my favourite routes for a Bristol RE journey were Eastern Counties services: Ipswich–Stradbroke (203), Ipswich–Bury St Edmunds (204), Ipswich–Colchester (207), Mistley–Ipswich (221/227), Ipswich–Aldeburgh (264), Ipswich–Norwich (851). Eastern National services: Harwich–Colchester (103/104), Harwich–Clacton (106). Eastern National/Eastern Counties joint service: Clacton–Ipswich (123). United Counties service: Cambridge–Biggleswade (175). United Counties/Eastern Counties joint service: Peterborough–Kettering (265). Carters Coach services: East Bergholt East End–Colchester (247), East Bergholt–Hadleigh–Colchester (755). Express Motors service: Caernarfon–Blaenau Ffestiniog (1). Badgerline services: Wells–Weston-super-Mare (126), Wells–Wincanton (160), Bristol–Wells–Yeovil (376). Northern Bus services: Sheffield–Dinnington (208/216/X50/X70).

On all these journeys, the Bristol REs never broke down. For Bristol Commercial Vehicles RE meant Rear Engine, but for me it meant Reliable Engineering!

In this book I have illustrated the Bristol RE in service from 1970 to 1994 in England and North Wales. This includes Tilling Group companies, National Bus Company subsidiaries, municipal operators, independents, plus some of the new companies created from the privatisation of the National Bus Company.

The first part of this book covers East Anglia, then we move to the South East and South West. After that we cross the north Midlands to Cheshire, North Wales and Greater Manchester. Then some of the last operators of the Bristol RE are covered, including Busways South Shields, Badgerline, and Northern Bus.

In researching information about the Bristol RE, I have been impressed by the number of Bristol REs in preservation that can be seen at bus rallies and running days. So, as a tribute to all the hard work, long hours, and expense needed to preserve and restore buses and coaches, at the end of this book are a few more recent images of Bristol REs in preservation.

Two abbreviations used throughout this book are ECW (Eastern Coach Works Ltd, Lowestoft) and NBC (National Bus Company).

Special thanks are due to my wife, Rosemary, for her support during the preparation of this book.

Robert Appleton

The bus that started my enthusiasm for the Bristol RE: Eastern Counties RS648 (KVF 648E) RESL6G with Eastern Coach Works forty-six-seat body, one of fourteen new in 1967. The location is Harwich Road, Mistley, with RS648 working a Mistley to Ipswich journey on service 221 in August 1970.

In 1968 Eastern Counties received twenty Bristol RELL6Gs with ECW fifty-three-seat bodies. These had five-speed semi-automatic transmission, which became the standard for all future Bristol RE deliveries. In October 1970 RL665 (PPW 665F), allocated to Saxmundham depot, was on loan to Ipswich depot. It is seen here after reversing off a stand at the Old Cattle Market bus station in Ipswich, departing on service 207 to Colchester.

Eastern Counties had fifteen dual-purpose Bristol RELL6Gs with ECW bodies and fifty semi-coach seats. They carried the coach livery when new in 1970, as shown by RLE875 (YAH 875J) at the Old Cattle Market bus station, in Ipswich, in July 1971. Next to RLE875 is RL675 (PPW 675F) dating from 1968.

Eastern Counties continued to receive new RL Class Bristol RELL6Gs with ECW fifty-three-seat bodies in the years 1969 to 1972. RL514 (EPW 514K) was one of thirteen new in 1972, seen on layover at the Old Cattle Market bus station at Ipswich in July 1972. The side advert shows why the fleet name was applied to the cream band.

Nine RL Class Bristol RELL6Gs with ECW fifty-three-seat bodies were new to Eastern Counties in 1969. These had the tall flat windscreen, as shown by RL706 (TVF 706G) at the Old Cattle Market bus station, in Ipswich, in September 1972. RL706 was allocated to Saxmundham depot and was about to depart on service 264 to Aldeburgh.

United Automobile Services 1224 (HHN 724D), on hire to Eastern Counties, at Ipswich Old Cattle Market bus station in September 1972. This Bristol RELH6G, new in 1966, had the express version of the ECW coach body, with bus-style destination display, and power-operated entrance door.

During the school half-term holiday in February 1971, the Eastern Counties seventy-seat Bristol FLF6G, allocated to East Bergholt outstation, was replaced by a forty-seven-seat Bristol RELH6G with ECW coach body. Here RE888 (GVF 888D) has arrived at East Bergholt outstation on the 14.35 service 209 from Ipswich.

Later, East Bergholt outstation exchanged RE888 for RE894 (SVF 894G), seen here at the Old Cattle Market bus station in Ipswich the next day, after arrival on 08.45 service 221 from Colchester. I had enjoyed the smooth and comfortable ride on RE894, helped by the air suspension, and, as RE894 was new in 1969, the five-speed semi-automatic gearbox.

The last Bristol REs delivered to Eastern Counties were eight Bristol RELH6Ls with ECW bus shell bodies and forty-nine semi-coach seats new in 1974. RLE741 (GCL 343N) was at Colchester bus station in July 1977, working National Express service 092 from London Victoria to Cromer.

Despite being painted in National Express livery, this RLE Class were used as dual-purpose vehicles. In contrast to the previous image, RLE744 (GCL 346N) was in the old Bishops Road bus station at Peterborough in April 1978, working on local bus service 330 to Glinton.

In 1966 Eastern Counties received eleven Bristol RELH6Gs with ECW coach bodies seating forty-seven. During 1967 RE890 (HAH 890D) was fitted with a Leyland 0.680H engine, and fully automatic transmission. In September 1979 RE890 was leaving Drummer Street bus station, in Cambridge, on National Express service 098, from London Victoria to Norwich.

RPU 869M was one of a pair of Bristol RELH6Gs, with the ECW Mark II coach body, ordered by Eastern National in 1974 but diverted to National Travel (South East). Transferred to Eastern Counties in 1978, RE849 was at Ipswich Old Cattle Market bus station on 11 October 1980, waiting to be crew operated on the 11.30 service 223 to Tattingstone.

The 1970-built Bristol RELL6G with ECW fifty semi-coach seats later received the NBC local coach livery of half poppy red and half white. Illustrated by RLE875 (YAH 875J) in Harwich Road, Mistley, working service 221 from Mistley to Ipswich in August 1974.

The Eastern Counties RLE Class, new in 1970, consisted of nine buses with the tall flat windscreen and six buses with the curved windscreen design. In contrast to RLE875 above, here is RLE863 (WNG 863H) at St Andrews Street North, in Bury St Edmunds, on 7 July 1981, working one of the Bury St Edmunds town services.

RS654 (KVF 654E), a Bristol RESL6G with ECW forty-six-seat body, was new in 1967. On 4 July 1981 the fourteen-year-old RS654 was parked at the old station yard in Cambridge, between Cambridge railway station and the Eastern Counties depot in Hills Road.

Eastern Counties RL680 (RAH 680F), a Bristol RELL6G with ECW fifty-three-seat body, was new to Ipswich depot in June 1968. On Sunday 25 August 1980, RL680 used the Manningtree level crossing whilst working 14.30 service 223 from Ipswich to Mistley. This journey was timed to take hospital visitors from Ipswich to St Mary's Hospital at Tattingstone.

Another of the 1968-built Bristol RELL6Gs was RL667 (PPW 667F). On 26 June 1982, RL667 was working from Saxmundham depot, seen at Ipswich Old Cattle Market bus station, prior to working 17.40 service 263 to Aldeburgh. Service 263 diverted from the normal 264 route to serve the village of Thorpeness north of Aldeburgh.

RLC718 (WPW 718H) was one of seven Bristol RELL6Gs with ECW forty-eight-seat dual-door bodies, new in 1969 and 1970 for Norwich City Services. RLC718 was rebuilt in 1972 to become a fifty-two-seat single-door RL. On 10 July 1982, RL718 had arrived at Surrey Street bus station, in Norwich, on service 872 from Saxmundham, where this service had connected with service 264, operating between Aldeburgh and Ipswich.

In 1981 Eastern Counties acquired nine Bristol RELL6Gs from Alder Valley. Their ECW bodies had forty-nine seats, with a large front nearside luggage pen. New in 1972, RL687 (DRX 631K) was at Surrey Street bus station, in Norwich, on 14 October 1983, carrying an offside advert for the Eastline network of limited-stop services.

On 2 January 1983, Eastline limited-stop service 792 from Ipswich to Cambridge was extended to Peterborough. The first journey from Peterborough was worked by RE853 (SAH 853M), a Bristol RELH6G with Plaxton Panorama Elite forty-nine-seat coach body, seen here arriving at Ipswich Old Cattle Market bus station.

Eastern Counties RL735 (AAH 735J) was a Bristol RELL6G, new in 1970. In September 1972, RL735 received this overall advert livery for the Eastern Counties Parcels Service, which she retained until transfer to Cambus in September 1984. On 21 April 1984, RL735 was seen at Queensgate bus station in Peterborough.

RLE743/744s (GCL 345/346N) received this bus livery in 1984. They were reclassified RL743/744 but retained the comfortable semi-coach seats. Allocated to Ramsey outstation, RL744 was departing from Queensgate bus station, in Peterborough, on 21 June 1984, working service 231 to Ramsey.

For many years the Eastern Counties outstation at Diss worked the first morning journey from Diss to Ipswich, and the last Ipswich to Diss journey in the early evening on service 851. On New Year's Day 1981, the Diss outstation bus RL738 (AAH 738J) had a day of rest at Diss bus park. This Bristol RELL6G was new in 1970.

Although officially allocated to Saxmundham, on 14 August 1983 Eastern Counties RL513 (EPW 513K), a Bristol RELL6G with Eastern Coach Works fifty-three-seat body, new in 1972, was at Stowmarket outstation. At that time, it was situated at the old goods yard at Stowmarket railway station.

Eastern Counties RL501 (APW 501J), a Bristol RELL6G with ECW fifty-three-seat body, was new to Ipswich depot in February 1971. On 20 June 1983, RL501 was working from East Bergholt outstation. At Mistley (Rigby Avenue) after working 17.35 service 221 from Ipswich, her next journey was the 18.35 service 221 home to East Bergholt.

Some of the dual-purpose RLE Class new in 1970 received overall poppy-red bus livery, but they retained the fifty semi-coach seats. On 7 April 1985, RL872 had worked 22.30 Ipswich–Hadleigh–East Bergholt service 205, and she was photographed the next morning at East Bergholt outstation. RL872 was on loan from Bury St Edmunds depot to Ipswich depot.

When Eastern Counties was split up in September 1984, nearly all coaching work passed to Ambassador Travel (Eastern Counties) Ltd. Ambassador Travel garaged coaches at several Eastern Counties depots. At Foundation Street depot, in Ipswich, on 29 October 1984, was ex-Eastern Counties RE848 (RPU 868M), a Bristol RELH6G with the ECW Mark II coach body. The Eastline livery had been applied during ownership by Eastern Counties.

Ambassador Travel RE860 (CAH 860K) at Foundation Street depot, in Ipswich, on 1 December 1984. This was one of the first batch of Plaxton Panorama Elite forty-nine-seat-bodied Bristol RELH6G coaches new to Eastern Counties in 1971.

The western area of Eastern Counties was transferred to a new company, Cambus Ltd, in September 1984. At Queensgate bus station, in Peterborough, on 28 September 1984, was Cambus RL521 (HPW 521L), a Bristol RELL6G with ECW fifty-three-seat body, new to Eastern Counties in 1972. RL521 was later renumbered 122 in the Cambus fleet.

Cambus RL505 (BVF 668J) on layover at the Acland Street coach and bus park at Peterborough, on 28 September 1984. RL505 was working from Oundle outstation on service 265 Kettering–Peterborough. This Bristol RELL6G, new to Eastern Counties in 1971, was later renumbered 116 in the Cambus fleet.

Cambus adopted a light-blue livery, as carried by 108 (XAH 873H) at the Acland Street coach and bus park in Peterborough, on 5 June 1985, after working in on service 343 from Whittlesey. This Bristol RELL6G, with ECW body, had fifty semi-coach seats, and was new to Eastern Counties as RLE873 in 1970.

Cambus 117 (BVF 822J) was a Bristol RELL6G with ECW fifty-three-seat body new to Eastern Counties in 1971 as RL506. On 29 March 1986, 117 was leaving Ely on service 116 from Newmarket to March.

Cambus 103 (TVF 705G) collecting passengers in Sidney Street, at Cambridge, on 30 August 1986. This Bristol RELL6G was new to Eastern Counties as RL705 in 1969. Thus 103 had the tall flat windscreen on her ECW fifty-three-seat bodywork.

A busy scene in Emmanuel Street, Cambridge, on 18 April 1987. Seventeen-year-old Cambus 109 (YNG 725J) was a Bristol RELL6G with Eastern Coach Works body, new to Eastern Counties in 1970 as RL725.

Cambus 150 (SAH 851M) at Queensgate bus station, in Peterborough, on 5 June 1985, prior to departure on the 12.35 service X47 to Leicester and Birmingham, a service that was worked jointly with Midland Red. 150 was a Bristol RELH6G with Plaxton Panorama Elite forty-nine-seat coachwork, new to Eastern Counties as RE851 in 1974.

All eight of the Bristol RELH6Ls with ECW forty-nine semi-coach seats in bus shell bodies, new in 1974 to Eastern Counties, received Gardner 6HLX engines in 1980/81. Thus, they were RELH6G when transferred to Cambus. On 3 January 1986, Cambus 157 (GCL 348N) was leaving Queensgate bus station, in Peterborough, on service 312 to Market Deeping.

Cambus 152 (GCL 343N) leaving Drummer Street bus station, in Cambridge, on 16 April 1987, working service X13 to Haverhill. Note that no National Bus Company symbols are carried. This was because Cambus had been privatised by the sale to its management on 8 December 1986.

On 17 April 1987, Cambus 154 (GCL 345N) was on layover at the Acland Street coach and bus park in Peterborough. As Eastern Counties RLE743 she received bus livery on repaint in 1984. A further repaint into Cambus bus livery followed.

A few Bristol RELL6Gs lasted long enough in the Cambus fleet to receive the revised Cambus livery. New to Eastern Counties as RL681 in 1968, Cambus 102 (RAH 681F) was in Emmanuel Street, Cambridge, on 3 March 1990. At the time, 102 was the oldest Bristol RE in the Cambus fleet.

On Sunday 24 July 1988, Cambus celebrated the 75th anniversary of the Peterborough Electric Traction Company commencing bus services. The running day included Bristol RELL6Gs operating the country bus services from Peterborough. Cambus 121 (HPW 518L) arrived in Peterborough on service 336 from Wisbech. 121 had been new to Eastern Counties as RL518 in 1972.

Eastern National had fifty-five Bristol RELL6Gs with ECW fifty-three-seat bodies. The first twenty, delivered in 1969, had the tall flat windscreens. In May 1971, 1512 (FVX 614H), from Colchester depot, was in Rigby Avenue, at Mistley, waiting to work the 09.10 service 70 to Colchester.

Service 123 Clacton–Ipswich, jointly operated by Eastern National and Eastern Counties, had a revised timetable in May 1970, which introduced more one-person operation. In June 1970, Eastern National 1505 (EPU 186G) pulled away from the bus stop at Church Lane in Brantham with a good load of passengers on the 10.45 Ipswich to Clacton journey.

The next thirty-five Bristol RELL6Gs delivered in 1970 to 1972 had the curved windscreen. New to Clacton depot in May 1970, Eastern National 1521 (HTW 179H) caught the evening sun at Harwich Road, Mistley, in June 1970, working the 18.15 Clacton–Ipswich 123.

Fresh from repaint, 1529 (LVX 117J) was on Station Approach at Harwich in September 1979. Allocated to Harwich depot, 1529 has the destination blind set for the works service from Harwich to the British Xylonite Plastics factory at Brantham. This service ran three times per day, seven days a week, for the shift changeovers at 06.00, 14.00, and 22.00.

1522 (KHK 414J) on the forecourt of Harwich depot on 30 August 1981. In 1980, the National Bus Company had decided that the white bands on single-deckers should be removed. Thus, 1522 had been repainted overall green, but even this livery cannot detract from the fine lines of a Bristol RELL6G with Eastern Coach Works body.

The Eastern National/Eastern Counties joint service 123 Clacton–Ipswich ceased on 29 April 1972. Happily, service 123 was reinstated on 15 June 1981. On 26 September 1981, 1504 (CVW 858G) had worked the 12.45 Clacton–Ipswich journey, and was collecting passengers at the Old Cattle Market bus station in Ipswich, before departing on the 14.35 journey home to Clacton.

In June 1982, service 123 was revised, meaning that the buses still worked complete journeys, but Eastern National drivers worked Clacton–Mistley, and Eastern Counties drivers worked Ipswich–Mistley. On 6 November 1982, Eastern National 1527 (LPU 452J) was having a driver change at Rigby Avenue, Mistley, whilst working the 08.40 Clacton–Ipswich journey.

Colchester depot had a works contract for day workers at the British Xylonite Plastics factory at Brantham. After working the morning journey on 29 October 1984, 1524 (KVX 570J) had run light to Mistley and was collecting passengers at Rigby Avenue to work the 08.45 service 87 back to Colchester via Manningtree, Lawford, Dedham, and Ardleigh.

1548 (WNO 548L) was from the last batch of Bristol RELL6Gs delivered to Eastern National in October/November 1972. On 5 February 1983, 1548 was working from Clacton depot, leaving Harwich bus station on the 10.35 service 106 journey to Clacton.

1404 (VHK 177L) was a Bristol RELH6G with the ECW Mk II coach body, new to Tillings Travel in 1972. Acquired by Eastern National in 1978 from National Travel (South East), 1404 was rebuilt by ECW in 1981 as the prototype for the new B51 coach body. In this form 1404 was at rest in Eastern Counties' Surrey Street depot, in Norwich, on 25 July 1981, after working Highwayman service 804 from Southend.

1408 (XOO 877L) was a Bristol RELH6G with Plaxton Panorama Elite forty-seven-seat body new to Eastern National in 1973. On 21 August 1982, 1408 was approaching the Old Cattle Market bus station in Ipswich, working Highwayman service 804 from Southend to Norwich.

1407 (XVW 632L) was new to Tillings Travel in 1973. It was acquired by Eastern National in 1978 from National Travel (South East). This Bristol RELH6G had a new Plaxton Supreme front fitted to her Plaxton Panorama Elite body in 1982. In this form, 1407 attended the Southend Bus Rally on 6 June 1982, where she was a fine ambassador for Eastern National's coaching activities.

1409 (X00 878L) was new to Eastern National in 1973. This Bristol RELH6G, with Plaxton Panorama Elite body, was converted into a wheelchair-accessible coach in October 1985 and renumbered 2203. Fitted with a nearside wheelchair lift, it was re-seated to seventeen seats plus nine wheelchair spaces. Allocated to Chelmsford depot, 2203 was at Colchester bus station on 5 October 1991.

Colchester Borough Transport bought fifteen Bristol RELL6Ls with ECW fifty-three-seat bodies. From the first batch of five new in 1972, 27 (SWC 27K) was departing from Colchester bus station in March 1978.

From the second batch of five delivered in April and May 1973, Colchester Borough Transport 14 (YWC 14L) and 15 (YWC 15L) were parked at the depot in Magdalen Street on 4 April 1981.

The final batch of five Bristol RELL6G with Eastern Coach Works bodies for Colchester Borough Transport were new in December 1973. From this batch 20 (OWC 720M) was in Colchester bus station in May 1977.

Late afternoon sunshine captured Colchester Borough Transport 24 (SWC 24K) in Colchester
bus station on 5 September 1981. After many subsequent owners, in 2014 SWC 24K was
purchased by Rob Sly for further preservation. Rob Sly is the author of the excellent Bristol
Commercial Vehicles Enthusiast website at www.bcv.robsly.com.

Ipswich Borough Transport did not buy any new Bristol REs. Instead, five Bristol RELL6Ls
with ECW dual-door forty-seven-seat bodies, new in 1969, were acquired from Leicester City
Transport in 1980. 122 (TRY 122H) was placed in service in Leicester livery, but with the
maroon band repainted cream. It is seen here at Tower Ramparts bus station, historically known
as Electric House, on 14 March 1981.

Ipswich Borough Transport 118 (TRY 118H) in Civic Drive, Ipswich, on 13 March 1982 with a good load of passengers. The Ipswich livery suited the ECW bodies on these Bristol RELL6L very well. Single-deckers were required for services 12 and 13 to the Chantry Estate due to the low railway bridge in Ancaster Road.

In 1987 TRY 118H passed from Ipswich Buses to Busways Travel Services in Tyne and Wear. It was rebuilt to single-door, refurbished, and repainted in Economic livery. Numbered 1802, TRY 118H was in service in South Shields on 15 October 1988.

ECU 201E was a Bristol RESL6L with ECW dual-door body, new to South Shields Corporation in 1967. Seating capacity was forty-five and this was achieved by having 3+2 seating at the rear. ECU 201E passed from Tyne and Wear Passenger Transport Executive to Bickers of Coddenham. With Bickers, ECU 201E was at the Blue Coat Boy terminus at Ipswich in April 1979, working the north Ipswich circular service 11.

G. W. Osborne and Sons of Tollesbury's UWX 368L on layover at Colchester bus station, on 27 December 1986, after working in on service 3 from Layer-de-la-Haye. This Bristol RELL6G with ECW fifty-three-seat body was new to West Yorkshire Road Car in 1973.

Charter Coach set up Coastal Red, which started operations on 1 September 1986, to take advantage of bus deregulation. Coastal Red operated from the Charter Coach depot at Great Oakley. On 7 July 1987, Coastal Red CRU 141L was working through Great Oakley on their commercial service 10 from Colchester to Harwich. CRU 141L was a Bristol RELL6G with ECW forty-five-seat dual-door body, new to Hants and Dorset in 1972.

Coastal Red also tendered successfully for some Essex County Council contracts. On 5 July 1987, Coastal Red LAE 348E was at Colchester bus station working Sunday service 129 to Clacton. LAE 348E was a Bristol RELL6L with ECW body, new to Bristol Omnibus Company in 1967.

LJB 422E of G. E. Dack and Son t/a Rosemary Coaches of Terrington St Clement was parked on the Ram Meadow coach park, at Bury St Edmunds, on 11 July 1981. This Bristol RELH6G with ECW coach body, to express specification, had power-operated doors and bus-style destination display. It was new to South Midland in 1967.

The last Bristol RELH to be built was this RELH6L with Plaxton Panorama Elite body, new to Davis of Harwood in May 1975. It was later owned by S & M Coaches of Benfleet. JNK 561N attended the Southend Bus Rally in June 1978, showing plenty of underfloor luggage space on the high-frame RELH chassis.

When British Leyland announced the closure of the Bristol factory, Viv Carter arranged a visit there using his Bristol RELH6G coach, SVF 896G. Here, SVF 896G stands alongside one of the last Bristol-built Leyland Olympian chassis at the factory on 17 September 1983. The two gentlemen are Bristol Commercial Vehicle managers Ron Cave and Brian Rickards, who made us most welcome. The factory closed in October 1983.

A rear view of SVF 896G, showing the classic ECW coach body, at the Bristol factory on 17 September 1983. SVF 896G was new to Eastern Counties in 1969 as RE896. Viv Carter acquired her in 1981 for preservation; it was also used to transport the Colchester Scout Band. SVF 896G made the long journey from East Bergholt to Bristol and back without any problems.

Viv and Valerie Carter formed Carters Coach Services in 1985. PWC 344K was a Bristol RELH6G with Plaxton Panorama Elite body, new in 1972 to Tillings Transport. After further service with National Travel (South East) and Eastern National, PWC 344K was acquired by Carters Coach Services. It is seen outside Manningtree High School in Colchester Road, Lawford, on 6 October 1986, working a school contract from Ardleigh to Manningtree High School.

Carters Coach Services' LWC 981J at Cattawade, on 7 July 1987, prior to working service 246 to Colchester via Brantham, East End, East Bergholt, Dedham, and Langham. LWC 981J was a Bristol RELH6G with Plaxton Panorama Elite body, new in 1971 to Eastern National. After further service with Tillings Transport, National Travel (South East), and Eastern Counties, she was acquired by Carters in 1987.

Carters Coach Services' XAH 872H in Station Road, Clacton, on 7 July 1987, heading to the departure stand to work the return journey on service 124 to Mistley. This was an Essex County Council-tendered service, running on Tuesdays, which was Clacton market day. XAH 872H was a Bristol RELL6G with ECW body, new to Eastern Counties as RLE872 in 1970.

DRX 631K was one of the nine Bristol RELL6G with ECW bodies acquired by Eastern Counties from Alder Valley in 1981. After withdrawal by Eastern Counties, Viv Carter rescued her from Ben Jordan's scrapyard and restored her to service. On 18 September 1987, DRX 631K worked service 247 from East Bergholt East End to Colchester, seen here leaving Colchester bus station to complete the journey to Colchester High Street.

United Counties 273 (ORP 273F) was a Bristol RELH6G with ECW forty-seven-seat coach body, new in 1968, seen here departing Bedford bus station on 17 July 1982, on a London to Corby working of express service 250. The yellow fleet number plate denoted allocation to Kettering depot.

United Counties was a keen user of the Bristol RELH6G with the ECW bus shell body and forty-nine semi-coach seats. 284 (TBD 284G) was new in 1969. Seen in Biggleswade, on 28 June 1980, after a very comfortable ride from Cambridge on service 175.

United Counties took further Bristol RELH6Gs with ECW bus shell bodies and forty-nine semi-coach seats in 1970, 1971, and 1973. 208 (YNV 208J) was one of the 1971 deliveries, seen here in Hitchin town centre on 17 August 1982.

New in 1968, United Counties 329 (RBD 329G) was a Bristol RELL6G with ECW fifty-three-seat body. It was photographed in Hitchin town centre on 17 August 1982. The blue fleet number plate with yellow edges denoted allocation to Huntingdon depot, so 329 was probably on loan to Luton or Hitchin depots at this time.

United Counties 342 (UBD 342H) was a Bristol RELL6G with ECW fifty-three-seat body. New in 1969, it was collecting passengers in Luton on 13 February 1982 whilst working service 43 from Luton to Hemel Hempstead. The brown fleet number plate denoted allocation to Luton depot.

United Counties 355 (VNV 355H) in Luton town centre on 23 January 1982. This Bristol RELL6G with ECW forty-six-seat dual-door bodywork was one of ten ordered by Luton Corporation but delivered to United Counties in 1970 after the takeover of Luton Corporation.

United Counties was split up on 1 January 1986, with the southern area becoming Luton and District with a new red and ivory livery. Transferred from United Counties and renumbered 393 in the Luton and District fleet, ANV 422J was a 1971-built Bristol RESL6G with ECW forty-seven-seat body. It is seen working a local service in Leighton Buzzard on 14 September 1987.

A Scottish interlude: Alexander (Fife) was the only Scottish operator to buy the Bristol RELL6G with ECW bus body, taking twelve in 1968, numbered FE21 to FE32. FE22 (JXA 922F) was at Kirkcaldy bus station in August 1970.

The Bristol REMH6G, with Alexander M-type coach body, was developed for the Scotland–London overnight express services of Scottish Omnibuses (Eastern Scottish) and Western SMT. These coaches were 12 metres (39 feet) long, with forty-two reclining seats, and a toilet compartment in the offside rear. Western SMT T2350 (TSD 131J), new in 1971, attended the Showbus rally at Hillingdon in June 1979.

Aldershot & District 615 (UOU 615H) was a Bristol RELL6G with Marshall dual-door forty-six-seat body, new in 1970. In 1972, Aldershot & District was merged with Thames Valley to form Alder Valley. Renumbered 431 in the Alder Valley fleet, UOU 615H was in Guildford bus station on 9 August 1980.

In 1971, South Midland was transferred from Thames Valley to the control of City of Oxford Motor Services, and the Oxford South Midland fleet name was adopted. This can be seen on 87 (RBW 87M), a Bristol RELH6L with ECW bus shell body and forty-nine semi-coach seats, new in 1974. It was seen at Gloucester Green bus station, in Oxford, on 14 June 1980.

City of Oxford Motor Services also bought Bristol RELH6Ls with the ECW Mk II coach body. New in 1974, 89 (RBW 89W) had arrived at Gloucester Green bus station in Oxford on 14 August 1982. It is seen working one of the express services from London (Victoria).

622 (XLJ 727K) was a Bristol RELL6G with fifty semi-coach seats in its ECW body, new to Wilts & Dorset in 1972. Later the same year, Wilts & Dorset was absorbed by Hants & Dorset. On 8 October 1981, 622 was at Salisbury bus station displaying both the Hants & Dorset and Wiltsway local identity fleet names.

The Bristol RELL6L with ECW dual-door forty-four-seat body became a Bristol Omnibus Company standard. 1205 (YHY 585J) was new in 1971. Seen here in service, in Gloucester, on 3 October 1980. Note the Gloucester fleet name and City of Gloucester coat of arms.

Bristol Omnibus Company 2050 (NHW 304F) was a Bristol RELH6L with forty-seven seats in its ECW coach body. On 3 October 1980, 2050 was backing off the stands at Gloucester bus station on a service to Bristol.

New in 1972, Bristol Omnibus Company 2069 (GHY 131K) was a Bristol RELH6L with forty-nine semi-coach seats in the ECW bus shell body. On 14 April 1982, 2069 was leaving Marlborough Street bus and coach station in Bristol on a service to Bath.

1419 (RDV 419H) was a Bristol RELH6G with forty-five-seat ECW coach body, new to Western National in 1970. Later transferred to Southern National, on 21 June 1992, 1419 had travelled from Taunton to Bristol to attend the Bristol Harbourside Rally.

NUF 438G was a Bristol RELL6G with Marshall body, new to Southdown in 1969. In 1981 she was acquired by Ray Cuff of Piddletrenthide in Dorset. On 2 October 1981, NUF 438G was in Yeovil bus station prior to working service 1 to Sturminster Newton. In the best traditions of country bus operation, passengers can wait seated on the bus prior to departure.

TCD 490J was new to Southdown in 1970. It was a Bristol RESL6L with Marshall forty-five-seat body. Later she spent nearly three years with Wealden Beeline of Five Oak Green, in Kent, from 1988 to 1991. On 14 April 1990, TCD 490J was working in Tunbridge Wells.

New to Trent in 1972, PCH 419L was a Bristol RELH6L with forty-nine seats in the ECW Mk II coach body. Acquired by Kent Coach Tours in 1986, on 29 September 1989, PCH 419L was leaving Faversham on service 666 to Ashford.

Bexhill Bus Company PLJ 742G, leaving Hastings for Bexhill on 28 September 1989. PLJ 742G was a Bristol RELL6G with ECW dual-door forty-five-seat body, new to Hants & Dorset in 1969.

Maidstone & District did not buy the Bristol RE; instead Leyland Panthers and Daimler Fleetline single-deckers were purchased. Hastings & District was split from Maidstone & District in 1983, and went on to purchase some second-hand Bristol REs. 465 (OCK 365K) RESL6L, with ECW forty-seven-seat body, was at Hastings railway station on 30 June 1989.

AHT 212J was new to Bristol Omnibus Company in 1971. It was a Bristol RELL6L with ECW dual-door forty-four-seat body. It was later rebuilt to single-door with fifty seats. Acquired by Hastings & District in 1989 and numbered 412, it is seen at Station Road, in Rye, on 30 June 1989.

Hastings & District 423 (PVT 223L) at Camber Sands on 28 September 1989. This Bristol RELL6L, with ECW fifty-seat body, was new to Potteries Motor Traction in 1973.

Lincolnshire Road Car 1225 (PFE 265K) at Newark-on-Trent bus station on 28 December 1983. 1225 was a Bristol RELL6G with Eastern Coach Works dual-door forty-four-seat body, new in 1972.

Lincolnshire Road Car 1213 (KHK 415J) was new to Eastern National in 1970. It was a Bristol RELL6G with ECW fifty-three-seat body. It was acquired by Lincolnshire Road Car in May 1983 and was seen at Newark-on-Trent bus station on 28 December 1983.

UEL 563J was a Bristol RELL6G with ECW body and fifty semi-coach seats, new to Hants & Dorset in 1971. Later she worked for Gash of Newark. When Gash of Newark ceased trading in May 1989, she was acquired by Lincolnshire Road Car, as seen in Newark-on-Trent on 1 July 1989. Note that the semi-coach seats have been replaced by bus seats.

LPU 452J is illustrated earlier in this book with its original owner, Eastern National. Acquired by Lincolnshire Road Car in 1983 and numbered 1214, LPU 452J was at Newark-on-Trent bus station on 29 September 1989. Both LPU 452J and UEL 563J, pictured previously, went on to see further service with Pennine Blue of Denton in Greater Manchester.

Trent 102 (YCH 891M) was a Bristol RELH6L with the ECW Mk II coach body with forty-nine seats, new in 1974. Seen in Chesterfield town centre on 17 June 1984, before working to Nottingham.

In 1972 the North Western Road Car Company based at Stockport was split up, with Buxton depot transferred to Trent. 285 (NCH 768M) was at Buxton Market Place on 28 July 1984. This Bristol RELH6L, with forty-nine semi-coach seats in the ECW bus shell body, was new to Trent in 1974.

J. H. Woolliscroft and Sons t/a Silver Service operated several Bristol RE buses. At their Baslow depot, on 12 June 1984, was PCW 202J, a Bristol RESL6L with Pennine Coachcraft forty-six-seat body, new to Burnley Colne & Nelson Joint Transport Committee in 1971.

Working for Silver Service at Chesterfield bus station, on 12 June 1984, was JEH 184K, a Bristol RESL6L with ECW forty-four-seat body, new to Potteries Motor Traction in 1972.

HTD 324K was a Bristol RESL6L with East Lancashire forty-seven-seat body, new to Darwen Corporation in 1971. After service with Blackburn Corporation and East Staffordshire District Council, HTD 324K saw further service with Stevensons of Uttoxeter, as seen in Burton upon Trent town centre on 23 August 1986.

Merthyr Tydfil Corporation took two batches of Bristol RESL. The 1973 batch were RESL6Gs with ECW forty-seven-seat bodies, illustrated by NHB 190M, seen in later life with Maun Buses of Mansfield, at Chesterfield bus station, on 27 March 1989.

The second batch for Merthyr Tydfil Corporation were RESL6Ls with East Lancashire forty-seven-seat bodies. One of these was KDW 706P, in service with Shearings of Wigan at Congleton, on 21 March 1987. It is seen whilst working services tendered by Cheshire County Council.

Lancashire United Transport (LUT) bought three batches of Bristol RESL6Gs. The last batch were new, in 1974, with Plaxton bodies and forty-one semi-coach seats, illustrated by 416 (TTB 447M), in St Helens, on 14 June 1984. LUT was fully absorbed by Greater Manchester Transport (GMT) in 1981, thus, 416 is in GMT livery but still working from the former LUT depot at Hindley.

The Runcorn Busway opened in 1971 and expanded to 14 miles of buses-only roads to serve the expanding new town part of Runcorn. Crosville operated T series routes on the Busway, with buses gaining an orange band and orange T on their NBC livery. On 14 June 1984, Crosville SRG186 (HFM 186J) was on the Busway at Runcorn Shopping City.

Also on 14 June 1984, Crosville SRG196 (HFM 196J) was on the Busway at Runcorn Shopping City. This batch of Bristol RELL6Gs were new in 1970 with ECW dual-door forty-eight-seat bodies.

Another good place to see Crosville's Bristol RELL6G was Crewe, where they worked on the K series of Crewe town services. On 15 June 1984, SRG203 (HFM 203J) was in Crewe town centre on service K1 to Leighton Park.

A rear view of Crosville SRG197 (HFM 197J), at Crewe bus station on 15 June 1984. SRG197 was a Bristol RELL6G with ECW dual-door forty-eight-seat body, new in 1970.

In 1972 Crosville received a batch of Bristol RELH6Ls with ECW Mk II forty-seven-seat coach bodies. Some were new in Crosville coach livery; others were new in NBC white coach livery. Later they received the NBC local coach livery and were reclassified from CRL to ERL. On 24 November 1984, ERL267 (TFM 267K) was parked outside Northwich depot.

This is sister vehicle ERL266 (TFM 266K) in a later Crosville livery. Town Lynx was the branding used for inter-urban express services. However, on 17 August 1985, ERL266 was at Northwich bus station working local service E29 to Winsford.

Crosville ERL290 (NFM 290M) working a local service in Congleton, Cheshire, on 14 July 1984. This Bristol RELL6L with ECW body had fifty semi-coach seats and was new in 1973.

Outside the Crosville office and bus station in Wrexham, on 17 August 1985, is Crosville ERL300 (BFM 300L), a Bristol RELH6L with Plaxton Panorama Elite body. When new in 1973, she carried NBC white coach livery with fleet number CRL300.

New in 1974, Crosville ERL305 (SFM 305M) was a Bristol RELH6L with ECW Mk II coach body and forty-seven seats. Seen at Chester Bus Interchange on 26 April 1986, working service C40 to Chester Zoo.

SJA 382K was new to North Western Road Car in 1971. It was a Bristol RELL6L with ECW body. In 1972, when North Western was split up, SJA382K transferred to Crosville, along with Northwich depot, receiving Crosville fleet number SRL247. At Northwich depot on 17 August 1985, SRL247 looked immaculate after a repaint back into North Western Road Car livery.

In September 1986, Crosville was split up, the Welsh operations becoming Crosville Wales. In Denbigh, on 25 April 1987, was Crosville Wales ERG280 (YFM 280L), a Bristol RELL6G with ECW body and fifty semi-coach seats, new in 1973.

In 1986, Gwynedd County Council decided that buses working their contracted network of bus services should carry a livery with a red front and a yellow band that separated the livery from the rest of the bus. Crosville Wales SRG179 (EFM 179H) was a Bristol RELL6G with ECW fifty-seat body, new in 1970, and was seen at Caernarfon bus station on 2 May 1987.

In September 1986 Ribble was split up, its southern area being transferred to a new North Western company. At the former Ribble depot, in Wigan, on 25 March 1988, were two Bristol RESL6Ls with ECW bodies, displaying the new North Western livery. OCK 356/363K were new to Ribble in 1972. Note the reversing window in the rear emergency door specified by some operators.

North Western 398 (HFM 213J) at Winsford depot on 5 March 1992. New to Crosville as SRG213 in 1971, this Bristol RELL6G had a long life because she was converted into a disabled people's bus with a wheelchair lift in the rear emergency door. SRG213 had transferred to North Western in 1990 with the Runcorn and Northwich depots of Crosville.

From deregulation day, 26 October 1986, Crosville did not register the Sunday journeys on service K38 Crewe–Macclesfield. Cheshire County Council put the Sunday service out to tender and awarded the contract to Potteries Motor Traction. On 2 November 1986, Potteries' 207 (PVT 207L) Bristol RESL6L, with ECW body, new in 1972, was at Macclesfield bus station waiting to return to Crewe.

Potteries Motor Traction opened a depot in Crewe to work services tendered by Cheshire County Council. On 12 February 1989, Potteries' 227 (PVT 227L) Bristol RELL6L, with ECW body, new in 1973, had just crossed the railway bridge near Crewe railway station.

JWU 335J was a Bristol RELL6G with ECW body and fifty semi-coach seats, new to West Yorkshire Road Car in 1971. On 2 May 1987, she was in service with Silver Star of Caernarfon at that town's bus station.

Cambrian Coaches of Tywyn's JEH 190K at Dolgellau, on 2 May 1987, working a former Crosville service S28 to Tywyn. JEH 190K was a Bristol RESL6L with ECW forty-four-seat body, new to Potteries Motor Traction in 1971.

Express Motors of Bontnewydd's TBD 278G is seen at Caernarfon bus station on 2 May 1987. This Bristol RELH6G, with ECW bus shell body and forty-nine semi-coach seats, was new to United Counties in 1969. I travelled on TBD 278G from Caernarfon to Blaenau Ffestiniog, a lovely ride. It was difficult to believe that this bus was eighteen years old.

ATA 764L was a Bristol RELL6G with ECW fifty-three-seat body, new to Western National in 1973. On 21 June 1988, she was working for Express Motors at Caernarfon bus station. Both ATA 764L and TBD 278G, illustrated previously, had the Bws Gwynedd red front and yellow band specified by Gwynedd County Council.

Several municipal operators in Lancashire and Cheshire bought Bristol REs because they could specify Leyland engines and remain loyal to East Lancashire of Blackburn for bodywork. Widnes Corporation Transport became Halton Borough Transport in 1974. On 14 June 1984, Halton's 2 (TTB 622L), a Bristol RESL6L with East Lancashire forty-two-seat dual-door body, new in 1972, was on layover in Widnes town centre.

Halton Borough Transport 10 (MCK 210P), a Bristol RELL6L with East Lancashire dual-door body and forty-seven semi-coach seats, new in 1975, was in St Helens town centre on 14 June 1984, waiting to work back to Widnes.

Devaway of Bretton (near Chester) RTF 307M at Northwich bus station on 4 May 1990 working service X2 Chester–Northwich under contract to Cheshire County Council. RTF 307M was a Bristol RELL6L with East Lancashire forty-eight-seat dual-door body, new to Widnes Corporation Transport in 1973 and acquired by Devaway in 1987.

Warrington Borough Council bought several Bristol REs. The last four, delivered in 1975 and 1976, had long lives with Warrington Borough Transport. They were RESL6Gs with East Lancashire forty-one-seat dual-door bodies. Seen here is 72 (LED 72P) at Golden Square bus station, in Warrington, on 7 May 1990. It had been rebuilt to single-door with forty semi-coach seats.

Seen here at dusk on 24 November 1989 is Warrington Borough Transport 71 (LED 71P), a Bristol RESL6G with East Lancashire body at Northwich bus station, waiting to work home to Warrington. 71 had been rebuilt from dual-door to single-door and fitted with forty-four bus seats.

Warrington Borough Transport purchased 88 (RVL 68L) from Lincoln City Transport; it was a Bristol RELL6L with Alexander forty-eight-seat bodywork new in 1973. On 5 March 1992 88 was working service 41 through Northwich to Greenbank College.

Rossendale Transport was the amalgamation of the Rawtenstall and Haslingden municipal operators. Opposite Rawtenstall bus station, on 29 August 1987, was 14 (JDK 914P), a Bristol RESL6L with East Lancashire forty-five-seat body new in 1975, advertising the Lancashire Bus Pass.

After bus deregulation, Rossendale Transport expanded services in to the Bury and Rochdale areas of Greater Manchester. 8 (YTC 308N), a Bristol RESL6L with East Lancashire forty-six-seat body new in 1974, was turning in to Rochdale bus station on 9 October 1988.

New to Eastern Counties as RL511 in 1972, this Bristol RELL6G with ECW body transferred to Cambus in 1984, where it was renumbered 118. Then, in 1987, EPW 511K entered service with the Lyntown Bus Company of Eccles, Greater Manchester. On 24 October 1987 EPW 511K was leaving Manchester city centre on service 27 to Eccles and Peel Green.

Lyntown Bus Company WSV 554 (EPW 515K), leaving the depot at Eccles on 22 November 1987. Another Bristol RELL6G, it was new to Eastern Counties in 1972 as RL515, then to Cambus, in 1987, as fleet number 119. Lyntown Bus Company ran a number of Bristol REs, mainly on services tendered by Greater Manchester Passenger Transport Executive.

Lyntown Bus Company WSV 553 (XAH 870H) picks up passengers in Eccles whilst working service 55 to Pendleton on 16 April 1988. New to Eastern Counties as RLE870 in 1970, then Cambus 106 in 1984, this Bristol RELL6G had retained its fifty semi-coach seats in the ECW body.

Lyntown Bus Company NUD 79M in Eccles town centre on 9 August 1988. This Bristol RELH6L with ECW body was new to City of Oxford in 1973. Instead of working express services from Oxford to London, NUD 79M was now running on local bus services in Greater Manchester, but the forty-nine semi-coach seats had been retained.

RPU 869M is illustrated earlier in this book with Eastern Counties. After further service with Ambassador Travel, RPU 869M came north in 1986 to work for Shearings of Wigan on local bus services. This Bristol RELH6G, with ECW Mk II coach body, was on layover at Ashton-under-Lyne bus station on 6 June 1992 with its next owner, Vale Coaches of Manchester.

When Greater Manchester Buses closed one of their depots in Tameside, six redundant bus drivers set up Pennine Blue in 1990. Their first service was 348 from Haughton Green to Mossley (Micklehurst). Pennine Blue built up an interesting fleet of Bristol REs, which were well presented, as shown by ex-Ribble OCK 354K, a Bristol RESL6L with ECW body at Ashton-under-Lyne bus station on 7 March 1990.

Also operating service 348 on 7 March 1990 was Pennine Blue SHN 73L, seen at Ashton-under-Lyne bus station. This Bristol RELH6G, with ECW bus shell body and forty-nine semi-coach seats, was new to United Automobile Services in 1973.

Pennine Blue KBL 228L at Ashton-under-Lyne bus station on 4 August 1990. This Bristol RELH6L with ECW Mk II coach body was new to Alder Valley in 1973. Note that its coach seats have been replaced by bus seats.

New in 1970 to Bristol Omnibus Company, Pennine Blue WHW 374H was in Ashton-under-Lyne bus station on 29 September 1990. WHW 374H was a Bristol RELH6L with ECW bus shell body and forty-nine semi-coach seats.

Pennine Blue YFM 272L on rail replacement duty at Altrincham railway station on 7 April 1991. This Bristol RELL6G with ECW body and fifty semi-coach seats was new to Crosville as ERG272 in 1973.

Also on rail replacement duty at Altrincham railway station on 7 April 1991 was Pennine Blue LTG 41L. This Bristol RESL6L with ECW forty-four-seat body was new to Aberdare Council in 1972. From 1988 to 1990 she saw service with Citybus in Belfast, being numbered 773. In this image LTG 41L was still in Citybus livery.

Pennine Blue UVL 874M departing from Hyde bus station to work back to Ashton-under-Lyne on service 346 on 11 April 1992. This Bristol RELL6L with Alexander forty-eight-seat body was new to Lincoln City Transport in 1973.

Pennine Blue OAE 961M on layover at Carrbrook, in the foothills of the Pennines, on 11 August 1992. This Bristol RELL6L with ECW fifty-seat body was new to Bristol Omnibus Company in 1973 with fleet number 1339, which was still carried nineteen years later.

The oldest Bristol RE that I saw in service with Pennine Blue was NLJ 821G, working service 428 from Ashton-under-Lyne to Failsworth on 15 June 1993. At the time it was fifteen years old and still going strong. NLJ 821G was a RELL6G with ECW dual-door forty-five-seat body. It was new to Hants & Dorset in 1968.

A visit to South Shields on 15 October 1988 was rewarded by the sight of Busways South Shields 1811 (YWC 18L) working hard with a near-full load of passengers. This Bristol RELL6L with ECW fifty-three-seat body was new to Colchester Borough Transport in May 1973.

Busways South Shields 1814 (OWC 723M), also in South Shields on 15 October 1988, was another Bristol RELL6L with ECW body and was new to Colchester Borough Transport in December 1973. Busways Travel Services had refurbished the Bristol REs acquired from different operators.

Merseyside Passenger Transport Executive was the only PTE to buy new Bristol REs. It bought twenty RESL6Ls with ECW forty-seven-seat bodies: ten in 1971, and ten in 1975. From the 1975 batch, 1825 (GTJ 385N) was working for Busways Travel Services in South Shields on 15 October 1988.

In August 1975 Thamesdown Transport took delivery of five Bristol RESL6Gs with ECW forty-three-seat bodies, numbered 166–170 (JMW 166–170P). These were the last Bristol REs to be bodied by Eastern Coach Works at Lowestoft. JMW 166P passed to Busways Travel Services, where it was renumbered 1817, and was in service at South Shields Market Place on 15 October 1988.

Another of the Thamesdown Transport Bristol RESL6Gs that passed to Busways Travel Services was 167 (JMW 167P), renumbered 1818 in the Busways fleet. 1818 gained Economic livery and was seen in service at South Shields on 15 October 1988.

Busways Travel Services faced competition from Hylton Castle Motors t/a Catch-A-Bus of East Bolden. On 15 October 1988, Catch-A-Bus HFM 218J was in service at South Shields. This Bristol RELL6G with ECW body was new to Crosville in 1971 with fleet number SRG218.

Hylton Castle Motors t/a Catch-A-Bus PDL 492H in South Shields on 15 October 1988. This Bristol RELL6G with ECW forty-nine-seat body was new to Southern Vectis in 1970.

Badgerline held a Bristol RE running day based in Wells on 15 June 1991. 1092 (RHT 141G), repainted in Tilling livery, was on layover at Yeovil bus station before returning to Wells. This Bristol RELL6L with ECW body was new to Bristol Omnibus Company in 1968, passing to Badgerline in January 1986 when the Bristol Omnibus Company was split up.

Badgerline 1257 (DAE 511K), a Bristol RELL6Lwith ECW body, was new in 1972. Originally a dual-door forty-four-seater for Bristol City services, it was later rebuilt to single-door with fifty seats. On 15 June 1991, 1257 had worked service 160 from Wells to Wincanton where the rain had set in!

Returning from Wincanton to Wells on 15 June 1991, 1092 (RHT 141G) was leading 1257 (DAE 511K). I was travelling on 1257, and this view shows a typical Bristol RE scene with effortless cruising in fifth gear.

In standard Badgerline livery, at Wells bus station, on 15 June 1991, is 1332 (OAE 954M). This Bristol RELL6L with ECW fifty-seat body was new to Bristol Omnibus Company in October 1973, passing to Badgerline in January 1986.

At the end of the Badgerline Bristol RE running day, on 15 June 1991, the sun shone on three Bristol RELLs at Wells bus station, showing three designs of ECW bodies: preserved Bristol Omnibus Company C1119 (UHU 221H), new in 1969, dual-door forty-four seats; preserved Wilts & Dorset 846 (TRU 947J), new in 1971 with fifty semi-coach seats; and Badgerline 1092 (RHT 141G), new in 1968 with fifty-three seats.

The Badgerline Bristol RE running day was repeated on 20 June 1992. Badgerline 1297 (EHU 391K) was working service 126 from Wells to Weston-super-Mare. It is seen here waiting in Axbridge for the bus from Weston-super-Mare to pass, due to the narrow streets in this village. 1297 was a Bristol RELL6L with ECW fifty-seat body new to Bristol Omnibus Company in 1972.

Badgerline 2071 (GHY 133K) arriving in Wells on 20 June 1992. This Bristol RELH6L with ECW body and forty-nine semi-coach seats was also new to Bristol Omnibus Company in 1972.

Badgerline 2071 (GHY 133K) attended the Bristol Harbourside Rally on 21 June 1992. This image shows the rear of the ECW bus shell body on the Bristol RELH chassis with the one-piece rear window, rear boot, and rear offside emergency exit door.

Northern Bus of North Anston held a Bristol RE running day on 12 September 1992. EVO 292J was a Bristol RELH6G with ECW body and forty-nine semi-coach seats, new to East Midland in 1971. Seen here at Dinnington bus station waiting to work to Sheffield.

HFM 594D was a Bristol RELL6G with ECW body and fifty semi-coach seats. It was new to Crosville in 1966 with fleet number ERG594. Restored by Northern Bus and repainted into Crosville dual-purpose livery, ERG594 was at Dinnington bus station during the Northern Bus running day on 12 September 1992.

A rear view of Northern Bus ex-Crosville ERG594 (HFM 594D) on 12 September 1992. This image shows the curved rear design of the original ECW body designed for the Bristol RE, before the peaked domes were introduced in 1967.

Northern Bus JHN 561K at Dinnington bus station on 12 September 1992. This Bristol RESL6G with ECW forty-five-seat body was new to United Automobile Services in 1972. JHN 561K later saw service with Citybus, in Belfast, from 1988 to 1991. It was then purchased for further service by Northern Bus.

In 1975 Fylde Borough Council purchased five Bristol RESL6Ls with ECW forty-four-seat bodies. One of them was HRN 105N, which was in service with Northern Bus at Dinnington bus station on 10 September 1994, during another Northern Bus Bristol RE running day.

XAH 873H was a Bristol RELL6G with ECW body and fifty semi-coach seats, new to Eastern Counties as RLE873 in 1970. She transferred to Cambus in 1984 and was later sold to Citybus, in Belfast, in 1988. In 1991 she was purchased by Northern Bus. On 10 September 1994, XAH 873H was at Sheffield Interchange during the Northern Bus Bristol RE running day.

United Automobile Services bought two batches of the 12-metre-long Bristol REMH6G with Plaxton Panorama Elite bodies. From the second batch that was new in 1973, 1316 (SHN 116L) was with Northern Bus at Dinnington on 10 September 1994, after working service X60 from Sheffield, which included a fast run on part of the M1 motorway.

Bristol Omnibus Company's Bristol RELL6L1003 (KHW 309E) was delivered in 1967 with the ECW single-door body. It was then rebuilt as a dual-door bus and allocated to the Cheltenham District fleet. In preservation, 1003 was at the Bristol Harbourside Rally, on 21 June 1992, in the care of the Cheltenham Bus Preservation Group.

Royal Blue livery on preserved Southern National 2365 (HDV 624E), a Bristol RELH6G with ECW coach body, new in 1967, at the Southend bus rally on 6 June 1981. Owned by Dean of Leatherhead at this time, and currently owned by Colin Billington for continued preservation.

Roger Downs' preserved Crosville CRG111 (AFM 111G) was a Bristol RELH6G with ECW coach body. It is seen here at the Manchester Velodrome on 7 May 2000 during a celebration of coaching event organised by the Greater Manchester Museum of Transport. Its livery is another that suited the elegant ECW coach body very well.

Liverpool Corporation were the only operator to buy Park Royal-bodied Bristol RELL6Gs; twenty-five were received in 1969 with forty-five-seat dual-door bodies. 2025 (SKB 695G) is preserved by the Merseyside Transport Trust and was photographed in Liverpool City Centre during a Trust running day on 12 September 2010.

Southern Vectis 863 (TDL 563K), a Bristol RELL6G with ECW body and forty-eight semi-coach seats, made several visits to the Isle of Wight when owned by Don and Sally McCririck. 863 was at Carisbrooke Castle on 31 July 2011 during a round the island tour to celebrate 863's fortieth birthday. 863 is now in the care of the Isle of Wight Bus and Coach Museum for continued preservation.

From 1976 to 1984 600 Bristol RELL6Gs with Alexander (Belfast) bodies were delivered to Citybus and Ulsterbus in Northern Ireland. Andy Cook's preserved Citybus 2526 (XOI 2526) attended the Clacton Bus Rally on 5 June 2016. In 2019, 2526 passed to Julian Patterson for continued preservation.

Dave Hales' preserved Eastern Counties RLE747 (GCL 349N), a Bristol RELH6G with ECW body new in 1974, recreated a short working from Ipswich to Tattingstone on Eastern Counties service 223 during the Ipswich Bus Rally on 9 April 2017. RLE747 is pictured at Tattingstone Church with the correct destination displayed.

David Edwards' preserved Eastern National 1516 (FWC 439H), a Bristol RELL6G with ECW body new in 1969, at Portman Road, in Ipswich, during the Ipswich Bus Rally on 9 April 2017. 1516 displayed a correct destination because Eastern National had short workings to Stratford St Mary on service 207, departing Colchester at 06.30 on Mondays to Fridays, and 22.30 on Saturdays, during the period 1961 to 1972.

Bibliography

Butler, Simon, *The Bristol RE A Family Profile* (Trevellan Books).

Curtis, Martin, *Bus Monographs: 5: Bristol RE* (Ian Allan Ltd).

Palmer, Bob, *Eastern National Fleet Record Volume 1: 1964–1990* (Essex Bus Enthusiasts Group).

Roberts, Duncan, *Bristol RE 40 Years of Service* (NBC Books).

Fleet History of Ambassador Travel, Cambus and Viscount (PSV Circle). PSV Circle News Sheets (PSV Circle).

Terminus Magazines (Eastern Counties Omnibus Society, now Eastern Transport Collection Society).

http://bcv.robsly.com – Bristol Commercial Vehicle Enthusiasts by Rob Sly.